A Guide to Discipline

Revised Edition

Jeannette Galambos Stone
Sarah Lawrence College

National Association for the Education of Young Children
Washington, D.C.

Copyright© 1969; 1978 revised edition. Second printing, November 1979; third printing, May 1981; fourth printing, July 1983.

National Association for the Education of Young Children
1834 Connecticut Avenue, N.W.
Washington, DC 20009
Library of Congress Catalog Card Number: 70-85679
ISBN Catalog Number: 0-912674-62-8
NAEYC #302

Printed in the United States of America.

Photographs by
Steve Herzog, *p. 1*
Elaine M. Ward, *pp. 3, 12, 15, 16, 19, 22*
Diana S. Palting, *p. 5*
Richard E. Farkas, *p. 7*
Ellen Levine Ebert, *p. 9*
O. W. Harper, *p. 10*
Ann Marie Mott, *p. 11*
Gail Ellison, *p. 13*
Jean Berlfein, *pp. 17, 23*
Dwight Cendrowski, *p. 18*
Peter Merom, *p. 20*
Peter W. Morris, *p. 25*
Rod Gilbert, *p. 29*

Contents

What Is Discipline?

Caring deeply about children means you want good control
and firm discipline for them.

What Is Discipline?

This is a book about teaching children to respect themselves and others and to show that respect. It is a book about having control of children in a variety of child care settings or in their homes and about teaching children to take over this control for themselves. It is not a book about punishment of children although it does talk about control.

Adults in this book will at times be called *teachers*. All adults who come in contact with children contribute to those children's education and are teachers whether they are called by that term or not—parents, bus drivers, caregivers, cooks, head teachers, volunteers, assistants.

When children do what they have been told not to do, they are acting disobediently. Some adults strike back with a word or a blow to the disobedient child. Others try reason. Still other adults ignore disobedience because they are indifferent or don't know what to do about it.

There are as many methods for disciplining children as there are adults. Some believe that sparing the rod spoils the child. They may say that if you really care about children, you control children in child care programs just as you would your own children at home,

and that failure to control them is failure of the whole system. Of course, there are adults who use very harsh methods because instant obedience is all that matters to them. There are others, however, who feel that showing affection to children is so important that an angry word destroys the children's feelings about themselves and a physical blow would be unthinkable. This kind of adult may feel that it is important to be popular with children, and that one must always be patient and nice.

My point of view lies somewhere in the middle. I believe caring deeply about children means you want good-humored control and firm discipline for them. Caring and control are both necessary ingredients of all good teachers. I believe that children should be expected to obey adults, provided the adults are reasonable. Young children are not experienced enough, or emotionally mature enough, to be in charge of themselves over long periods of time. Therefore, they need to accept an adult being in charge of them. The more skillful we as teachers are, and the more we understand children and how long it takes to grow, the more thought we put into leading children from adult control to the development of their own inner control.

I believe discipline works best when we feel in charge because we like being with children and respect their need for security. It works when adults *really* mean it when we say each child is different and rightfully so. It works when adults are firm, watchful, and affectionate, not mean or wishy-washy. Although adults are in charge, I cannot agree with adults who hit or embarrass children in order to make them bend to their will. I think an adult's will should be based on sensitive tuning-in to children's faces and voices, not on some rigid set of rules no matter what.

I believe in discipline that feels strong not hard; kind not brutal; that holds children when they break loose not punishes by hitting back. I will try to explain these beliefs in detail in this book, using examples from everyday life with children.

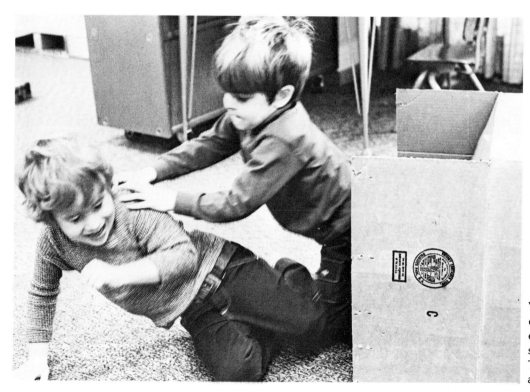

Young children are not experienced enough, or emotionally mature enough, to be in charge of themselves over long periods of time. Therefore, they need to accept an adult's being in charge of them.

All adults who come in contact with children contribute to those children's education and are teachers whether or not they are called by that name.

Would I Like Myself as a Teacher?

Would I Like Myself as a Teacher?

Few of us can honestly say we never have trouble getting children to "mind." All of us have good days when the children like themselves and each other and enjoy life. Most of us also have days when we feel the children are miserable, and getting them to behave well is a hard job. We feel we have been too cross or too easy. We feel discouraged. Most of us have high ideals, but we sometimes find ourselves too tired, or the children too unhappy, to fit the ideal. We search for solutions.

Young children need action. As they grow and learn, children move, touching and testing everything around them. They want attention and praise. They act babyish and uncontrolled one day and grown-up the next. It is natural for them to behave in those ways. But it is in the nature of life around them that they need to develop control of themselves and accept discipline. Spontaneous behavior in small children can be pleasing, of course. They can listen and obey and share. Often, however, they behave just the opposite—they are silly, noisy, selfish, or cry or act uneasy.

The job for us is to develop a way to teach children without demanding instant perfection or giving in to every whim. Good teachers do not force such slavish obedience that they break children's spirits. Nor do they constantly give in and set no limits at all for children. How do teachers develop discipline without being too weak or too tough? What is fair, and what is unfair and mean?

We do not want children to think that anything goes, just because we want to be friendly. We do not want them to be silent and afraid of us. The world needs people who grow up full of courage and original ideas, not people who are timid and simply nice. The time for people to develop resourcefulness is in their early years. Children can feel strong and self-confident in their first group experiences and at the same time respect the adults and other children in the group.

Children learn both social and cognitive skills best *if they learn self-esteem at the same time.* Children who like themselves and feel esteemed by others do not have to act rebellious or sullen. Children, like adults, do not feel like doing much if they are squelched or put down. If they are treated with disdain rather than respect, they hit back. However, if their safety and needs are taken seriously, they feel responsible and free, then, to interest themselves in a variety of activities.

This means that discipline depends in part on adults' *own* skills and good conduct. It depends on whether our teaching combines caring with control.

This is hard, especially with difficult children. It demands a lot of us. Good discipline is not just punishing or enforcing rules. It is liking children and letting them see that they are liked. It is caring enough about them to provide good, clear rules for their protection.

As you look at yourself and your teaching methods, if may help to ask these questions: Would I like to attend this program myself? Would I like myself as a teacher?

They are painful questions if you have had a long hard day, if you have been quick-tempered or over-permissive, or if the children have been unruly or rude. But if you have had a good day and been able to be fair and firm and caring, then you can feel satisfied with yourself and your job.

Whether you feel good or discouraged about yourself at the end of the day, though, there is always the task of getting ready for the next day.

Children learn both social and cognitive skills best if they learn self-esteem at the same time.

What Can I Do,
In Advance,
To Avoid Problems?

If children know that what they do is important to the adult, it starts being important to them too.

What Can I Do, In Advance, To Avoid Problems?

Give Yourself Plenty of Time

One simple but crucial component of good discipline is to begin the day early enough at home so you arrive at the center or school well ahead of the first child. If you plan interesting and stimulating things for children to do, if you have time to help other staff members set up the rooms, then you and the staff are ready to greet children as they arrive. This greeting, with warm interest in each of the children, shows them that they matter to you and are important people. Also, it lets them know that what they do and the way they act are important to you.

Discipline is based exactly on this: *If children know that what they do is important to the adult, it starts being important to them too, especially if the child and adult like and respect each other.* It becomes important to children to keep busy, finish projects, get along with others, help keep the room in order, engage in conversations, listen to stories, and play

peacefully and with concentration when alone. These things start being important to the child (if they are for the adult) the minute he or she steps inside the room.

Children may feel troubled, maybe because of a hard time at home, or while recovering from an illness. But as they arrive, they soon know whether or not they will find *affectionate care, reasonable order,*

Greeting children with warm interest shows them that they matter to you and are important people.

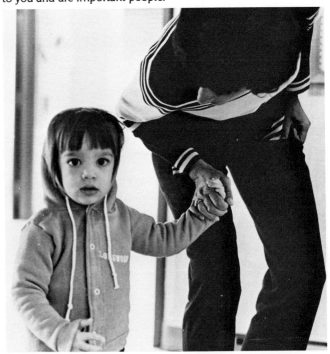

security, and an interesting day—child care setting qualities that help children to be "good" and develop self-control. Not punishment, not fear, not tension, not silence, not softness, not pity.

If you are poorly prepared or not working well with other staff members, if you feel rushed, or if you dread the day ahead, children sense this tension or disorder or boredom when they arrive. Often they misbehave as a result. A good child care program works better if the atmosphere is pleasant—not tense or bristling. Every staff has problems, but maybe these can be set aside while children are present. Time at the beginning of the day is essential for getting off to a good start.

Plan a Good Program

One way to prevent problems is to plan a daily program that is suitable for the ages and needs of the children you serve. If you don't know how to plan, you will want to learn more about Head Start centers, family child care, nursery schools, child care centers, co-ops, and kindergarten and primary programs. Your local school, library, governmental agencies, and Affiliate Group of the National Association for the Education of Young Children offer many services to people working with young children. You can take courses, observe other child

Young children need plenty of time to play and learn through their own ideas. It is important to have materials in places that will make it easy for the children to use them.

care programs, talk to a supervisor, or attend conferences or workshops.

For one thing, young children need plenty of time to play and learn (with gentle supervision) through their own ideas with their own selection of materials. Pretending to be parents in the housekeeping corner, construction workers by using blocks, and other similar dramatic play activities are favorites of young children. Exploring art, looking at books, working puzzles, creating music, and other ways of investigating and manipulating their world are also extremely important to children. There can also be some time when children are involved in other learning activities under the direction of the grownups.

Children who have problems often feel more peaceful and cooperative after working with clay or water or sand. They also need plenty of hard physical play inside and outdoors. Sometimes you may want to plan a special activity for a child in difficulty. An adult who can help these children individually may also be necessary.

Children can be counted on to act their age. If the program is too formal, so that younger children are expected to act like older ones, they feel anxious or rebellious. They misbehave if they are asked to sit still at tables or desks for very long or if adults make them stand in line or if they cannot talk or move around the room. Also, young children misbehave if they are forced to do things that are too hard—things that adults end up doing while the children just watch. Four-year-old children need things to do that are just right for four-year-olds. Our goal is for young children to accomplish what *they* can do.

Check to See How the Room Respects the Children

Children from varied cultural groups may feel most comfortable in familiar types of rooms. Some will be used to physical closeness with many people. Others will find larger, quieter rooms more like their homes. Providing pictures, books, and dolls, for example, which match various family backgrounds, shows respect for the children. Room and space need adept arranging. Children who feel at ease will be more likely to accept adult control as they

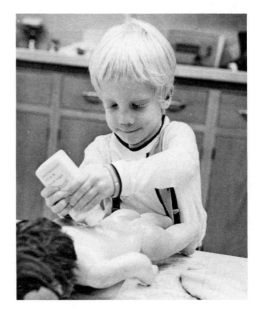

Children who feel at ease will be more likely to accept adult control as they learn self-control.

learn self-control.

Blocks, paints, crayons, scissors and paste, wood-working tools, dolls and dressup clothes, water, puzzles, swings, climbers, and sand—all of these help all children grow and learn, whether they are rich or poor, whether from suburbs, farms, or cities.

It is important to have these materials in places that will make it easy for the children to use them. Puzzles on shelves low enough so pieces won't be dumped, easels with floor coverings underneath to catch paint spills, real woodworking tools with soft wood—all help children be more successful.

Children find waiting to use supplies or sharing them with others difficult. Providing enough supplies will help children stay interested in what they are doing.

Storing things where children can choose and return items on their own is also important. Things for adults only are best stored where children will not be able to get them.

You will probably want to check your room each day to see whether it is set up to provide as many ways as possible for children to grow and learn.

Providing enough supplies will help children stay interested in what they are doing.

Your Manner Affects Children's Behavior

Adults set the example for good behavior, and we know that children cannot follow our good example if we are setting a bad one!

Your Manner Affects Children's Behavior

C hildren may arrive each morning feeling peaceful, but they will begin to misbehave if they are
bossed and herded around rather than treated
like decent human beings. Children imitate adult
examples. If an adult is harsh or teasing, harsh or teasing children are the result. An adult who combines
caring with fair and steady rules sets an example also.
Children who are treated this way tend to be cooperative.

It must be said, however, that children vary a great
deal. Skilled adults notice, for example, that to be most
effective a rule may need to be stated in a soft voice
for one child and in a louder tone for another or for a
whole group. Some children respond to a silent ges-
ture to sit down, and others need a clear "Please sit
down." *Just as adults are individuals with special
needs, children deserve to be treated in ways that are
best for them as individuals.*

An adult who combines caring with fair and steady rules sets an
example also. Children who are treated this way tend to be
cooperative.

But Problems Are Sure to Occur

Adults can often use their voices, hands, faces, and actions as tools for maintaining control and keeping a lot of problems from happening.

17

But Problems Are
Sure to Occur

Not all adults react in the same way to children's problems, and what is a crisis to one adult may be easily handled by another adult. Children who talk and move around or act sad or cry or speak loudly are easily accepted by adults who know what it is like to be a child. There are situations, though, that almost always cause adults (no matter how skilled they are) to ask, "What do you do when . . . ?"

What do you do when children run around the room, knocking into people and things? First, you try to understand why the children are behaving this way as you settle them down. Understanding does not have to be a long, slow process; it can happen at lightning speed. Children may act wild and restless because they are hungry or scared or excited by what they see in the room or because they are just feeling high. Adults who respond with anger and loud voices may excite children and speed them up just when the aim is to get them to stop and focus on something.

It works well for adults to greet overexcited children with a firm hand as they come into the room. You can speak to them kindly, with authority, and with some direction about what they should do first. You might

ask whether they would like to start the day building with blocks or working at the water table. Or you can simply take a galloping child by the hand or put an arm around the child and say, "No more running for now. I want you to play over here for a little while." You can lead the child there, sit down together, and create as much interest in the activity for the child as you can. In this way, one adult can usually redirect two or three restless children at once.

You will often find that the rough, runabout child calms down gradually and proceeds to work independently. Sometimes, though, a restless child must be guided in this manner through an entire day. If you have more than one such child, you may need extra

Adults who respond with anger and loud voices may excite children and speed the children up just when the aim is to get them to stop and focus on something.

adults to assist you. Many teachers find volunteer help for assistance.

It may sound unfair for one or two children to get a lot of attention, but it is not unfair, because *all* children learn from what goes on between one adult and one child. If you settle down one restless child, or befriend a shy one, all those present will learn that you take good care of children. The children will feel that you are in charge and that they are safe with you. They will learn some ways of handling problems, too. Of course, if you use sarcasm or physical force, they learn something else—that you are someone to tease or fear. But if you keep calm, fair, loving, and strong, they learn to trust you and cooperate with you.

What do you do when children just stand around and refuse to join in? What is happening inside these children? Can we play our hunches, quickly? Such children might not be feeling well; have been scolded or punished at home; have seen or heard something scary; or feel inferior. Whatever it is, they do not gain courage when people point at or embarrass them or try too hard to coax them. They probably feel better able to respond to adults who simply accept them the way they are, who move about with an air of gentle control, who make it clear they will help if the children want help, and who do not press but do not neglect them. The child will usually respond when you say, "If you want to watch for awhile, that's OK . . . and if you need help or want to talk, I'll be right here." In other words, good teachers move with the grain not against it.

What do you do when children refuse to join in?

Skilled adults do not waste their breath talking, scolding, or explaining when children cannot really listen.

What do you do when a child spits? No time to guess about causes until later, because spitting often builds up fast to outbursts of wild aggression. The quickest, fairest, calmest way to deal with this is to stop the child (without hurting) and announce, "I will not let you spit on anybody. If you have to spit, do it in the sink (or in this dish or over here in this corner of the yard)." No scolding is necessary; it probably will not be effective anyhow. Tell children firmly *where* they can spit, but that they cannot spit at people.

What do you do about hitting, kicking, scratching, attacking? Again the adult must state the rules. "I cannot let you hit people. If you have to hit, then bang on the floor (or punching bag or lump of clay). I know how you feel, but I cannot let you hurt people, and I cannot let them hurt you." That's that. You can kneel down and talk to the child directly while looking into his or her eyes, holding the child if necessary.

Some children may have to be held or carried or allowed to thrash around away from the other children (who will need to be reassured by another adult). These storms pass, though, and skilled adults do not waste their breath talking, scolding, or explaining when children cannot really listen. You can stay nearby, do not panic, do not rage back at the child, but simply remain firm in your stand: No hurting is allowed. When the child has quieted down—and it may take a long time—you can put an arm around and reassure the child that it will be all right. You can tell the child you are willing to listen. You may say that you keep children safe and that is why you had to stop the hitting. You may add that people have hard times but that you think the child now feels better and will have a better time for the rest of the day.

Biting is considered, by some, to be the worst thing a child can do. Biting is dangerous, and it frightens both the biter and the bitten person. The adult first separates the two children. You can comfort the bitten child and make sure that he or she is all right, receiving first aid if necessary. You may need another adult to help, because you will want to stay with the biter, making it clear immediately and firmly that you will not allow biting of people. "I will not permit biting. It is dangerous. I want children to be safe here." You can assure the biter that you will not let harm come to anyone. A soothing activity like water play or a favorite puzzle can be given to the child. The hurt child must also be comforted and then interested in something else.

It does no good to encourage other children to bite back to show how it feels. Biting is wrong because it is powerfully destructive and dangerous. Since it is wrong, it is wrong for everyone at all times.

Do you ever punish a child? We are adults talking about teaching children. Spanking or isolation or shaking or angry shouting at children have no place in teaching anything. When adults hit children to get them to mind, too much has already gone wrong, and discipline has broken down. The best teachers in the world get so angry or frustrated at times, though, that they reach an emotional breaking point. Afterwards,

they wonder just where the situation got out of hand and how to live with themselves.

Most adults do not like themselves after they hit a child. They may make excuses by saying that it was the only way to make the child stop misbehaving. And they feel relieved because children *can* make us angry enough to hit. At the same time, they feel deep within that a big person should not hit a small person. Adults set the example for good behavior, and we know that children cannot follow our good example if we are setting a bad one!

Therefore, you do not hit children when you want them to stop hitting. You do not yell at children to get them to stop yelling, or spit at children to indicate they should not spit. Of course, you want children to know how to sympathize with others and to know how it feels, but you have to show them *how to act,* not how *not* to act. If you were to teach only by copying children's bad behavior to show them how it feels, you would knock down their block buildings, tear up easel paintings, cry when they cry, and so on. If you did these things, you would become a child when what children need most is an adult. They need an adult who is trustworthy, who is in charge of them, and who has self-control.

There are effective and decent ways to conduct yourself during a child's explosive outburst, without becoming childish. Use your hands and arms and body to hold the child in your arms or in a small room with you. The child will benefit by your control and by your understanding, will finish with the outbreak, and be all right. The child will remember, next time angry feelings come up, that you are not an enemy and that you have ways to help establish self-control. And you will not have hit the child.

The difference between stopping children by hitting or by holding is tremendous. When adults hit, they take very unfair advantage of children. But when you hold, you are protecting as well as controlling the child. These are two very different methods, even though the holding may have a fairly physical look to it. Occasionally, you may find it necessary to hold children's arms if they try to strike you, or grasp their chins if they try to bite you, or place your ankle over their legs if they try to kick you. If you do this only to control children's actions, because you believe that it would be wrong to strike them, they are safe and you are safe. Both of you will come out of the crisis able to work together and with respect for each other.

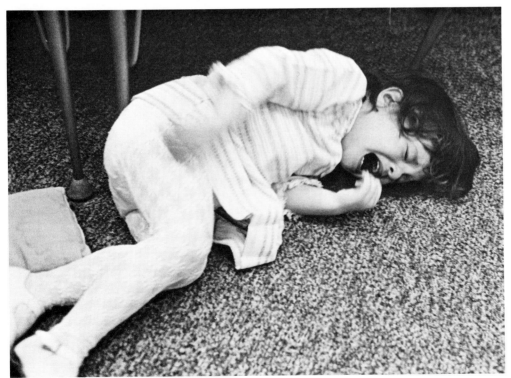

Spanking or isolation or shaking or angry shouting at children have no place in teaching anything. There are effective and decent ways to conduct yourself during a child's explosive outburst, without becoming childish.

Talking with Children:
What to Say,
How to Say It

Your words can help children understand their feelings and the feelings of other people too.

Talking with Children:
What to Say,
How to Say It

We have been discussing the use of physical restraint when childen get supercharged, but things are not usually that violent. Adults can often use their voices as tools for maintaining control and preventing many problems in the first place.

When things are going well, your voice can be soft, natural, and casual. When you sense a need for more control in a child or a group, your voice ought to take on a firm tone that seems to say, "All right, now, take it easy, slow down." In fact, you can *say* things like: "*Tell* her what you want." "*Think* about what you are doing." "*Careful!* Let's not get too silly." Your voice and direct words can bring mischief to a quick halt.

Often your hands, face, and bodily actions are needed to emphasize words like those examples above. You need to get over to troubled children, not call across the room. You need to squat or kneel down, talk directly to children, look kindly and intently into their eyes, reach out and take gentle hold of their arms or shoulders or sit down right there to talk out the difficulty. The situation begins to cool from the boiling point.

If a whole group of children breaks out into misbehavior, your voice needs to rise to cover the room sounds. Now you can boom out, not shrilly or nastily, but *out.* Let everyone hear what you are saying. If you speak softly and warmly most of the time, now that your voice is resounding children will listen, knowing that you require their attention for something important.

In spite of our best intentions, though, it is easy to let our voices betray our true feelings about behavior that upsets us. With each day's problems, it is necessary to hang tight to all you know and not plunge into some other way that suddenly looks better. Many times adults who have basic good sense and patience get off the track in their attempts to manage difficult children or to just try to generally keep things running smoothly.

Adults' Voices

Some adults who talk with young children adopt an extra sweet voice. It is high-pitched and sticky, and sounds phony to everybody, especially to the children. It invites false answers and tuning-out. Or they may take on a let's-be-pals voice. However, it is too superficial and intimate. Children cannot trust such adults to mean what they say. Or you may hear an adult lay down the law in a hard, harsh voice that sounds aggressive and frightening, causing children to tense up, withdraw, or hit back. Tension

and fear have a terrible effect on children, even though they may make children be still. No better is the weary tone of the martyr-teacher, with long explanations and patience-through-gritted-teeth. This comes across to the children as disgust with them. It causes children to feel explosive, and to test limits.

When we find ourselves sounding superficial or mean or weak in our own ears, we need to stop and listen and look. Listen to ourselves, and then look to see what our mistakes have been and what our strengths are. Most importantly, we need to look hard to see what the children's faces and behavior are telling us.

Skilled Ways of Talking to Children

The following is some adult talk that you hear good teachers and parents use to teach children how to discipline themselves. The words help children understand their feelings and the feelings of other people, too. Of course, these are only examples that carry the ideas adults want to get across to children. You will have your own way of saying these things.

You need to squat or kneel down, talk directly to children, look kindly and intently into their eyes, reach out and take gentle hold of their arms or shoulders, or sit down right there to talk out the difficulty.

VISTA

Spiderman is too rough and loud for inside. When we go outside, we'll find a place for you to play that game.

It's hard for Meredith to wait so long for a turn. Let her have the truck in about three minutes. I'll time it on my watch and let you know.

Some children like to draw designs, Lisa. Other people like to draw people and houses. It's up to each person.

It bothers me when you call Kevin stupid. He is not stupid. He's playing in his own way, and that's fine.

It's all right for Dana to be over there by himself, Elena. Sometimes people need to be alone.

I don't want you to laugh when someone gets hurt. Tom's hand really hurts, and that can be scary, can't it? Luis, would you bring the tissue box to Tom? Thank you.

Yes, you can write your own name, but Jonathon does not have to if he'd rather not.

I know you want to be the father. We could have two fathers in this house . . . We need a grandfather, too, and some uncles.

I know how you feel, Juan. It is hard for you. But I think we can work it out.

Please don't call Killian a baby. He is four years old. It's just hard for him to get used to being without his mother.

Alicia, your loud crying makes it hard for us to hear each other. (To the other children) When she can tell me with words what's the matter, she will.

I cannot let you hit him—it hurts. *Tell* him. Tell him with words.

Yes, I heard Lara say that word. Lara, we've heard that word enough. It's not a school word.

Tony, the children worked hard making their block building; they're angry that you knocked it down. Let's help build the tower back up. Then you can build something of your own.

Keep the sand down low, this way. Dig down with the shovel.

People don't like it when you grab. Ask and then listen to the answer. Did she say no? OK. Let's see what else you can find to do.

I won't let you kick me, and I won't kick you either. My job is to make this a safe place for all of us.

Screaming won't get you a turn, Ann. Terry needs more time on the swing. Then I'll help you get your turn.

Sean, the children want to hear the story. Tell me at the end of the book.

Do you want to come back to the story, Sean? Good! Here is a place for you. Listen . . .

Paint here on your own paper; Susan does not want you to paint on hers. Would you like a larger piece of paper?

Maricela, I don't want you to dump the puzzle all over the floor. Let's both pick up the pieces and figure out how to do it together.

Off the tables, please . . . The climber out in the other room is good for climbing!

Bryan, please don't yell across the room. Walk over to your friends and speak right to them.

No pushing on the slide! First Tony, then Sue, then Lucinda, then Pete.

On this walk, I'll go first because I'm a grown-up. Ms. Allen will walk in back with Elton and Tina. No one is to run ahead. Walk so you can see my back.

I am not going to chase you, Celeste. Walk back here to me . . . take giant steps!

I know you don't want to stop what you are doing now, but your father is waiting. Would you like to use those pegs again tomorrow? Remind me.

I saw that you did not help put the trucks away, Lamont, after you had played with them. Next time, I'm going to ask you to help.

I know you brought that doll from home, Beatriz. It's beautiful. I'll help you show the doll to everybody, safely. Then we'll put it in a special place until it's time to go home.

Pour the orange juice carefully so it does not spill. Watch . . . There, that's just right.

Water on the floor is slippery and could make someone fall. Here's a mop for you to mop up over there . . . I'll sponge up here.

This sink is pretty small for four children. Let's fix another pan of water on this table . . . first a towel on the table, then the pan of soapy water . . . now an egg beater and pitchers and cans. Anything else?

We're going to make scrambled eggs today. There are two cooking tables; mine is here, and Mr. Klemach will be over at that table. If you don't want to cook, you can use those flannel boards over on the blue rug.

Yes, I know, Mari. But people don't all have to sing when we have music. Sometimes Tim likes to listen.

You can dance to this record in the space from the wall to that table. If you don't feel like dancing, you might watch or clap with the beat.

We got back from our trip to the music store early, so let's play one of the records we bought while we rest—over here on the rug.

I know you're mad. I understand. But shouting *that* loudly won't help. Come, let's talk about it.

Sam's drawing is his own idea. Each person's ideas are very important.

Where Do I
Go from Here?

We need to look hard to see what the children's faces and behavior are telling us.

Where Do I Go from Here?

Discipline is not just a word or a technique or a set of rules. We have been talking about the whole climate in working with young children and the ways adults behave toward children in good times and bad. Each of us has an ideal—the kind of person we want to be every day. Sometimes we succeed; other times we fail. Even as we keep the ideal as our guideline, we have trouble living up to it.

What happens? As adults working with very young human beings, you need an endless supply of understanding and energy to help children develop self-control. Let's think again about what you can do to teach children to feel and show respect for themselves and others.

Would I Like Myself as a Teacher? Good discipline combines caring and fairness with control.

What Can I Do, in Advance, to Avoid Problems? *Give yourself plenty of time* before the children arrive. A good child care program works better if the atmosphere is pleasant. *Plan a program* that is suitable for the ages and needs of the children you serve. *Check to see how the room looks to the children.* Children who feel at ease will be more likely to accept adult control as they learn self-control.

How Does My Manner Affect Children's Behavior? Children imitate adult examples. Children tend to be cooperative with adults who combine caring with fair and steady rules.

What Do I Do When Problems Occur? Some problems will require that you stop the child immediately. Others will best be handled if you first think about what is causing the problem. You will always want to speak kindly to children, with authority, and offer some direction about more appropriate behavior. Children need adults who are trustworthy, who are in charge of them, and who have self-control.

How Do I Talk with Children? Adults can often use their voices, hands, faces, and actions as tools for maintaining control and preventing problems. Your words can help children understand their feelings and the feelings of other people, too.

Where Can I Go from Here? Try out some of the ideas that you have been thinking about as you read this book. How can you use them to best work with the children you know?

Information about NAEYC

NAEYC is . . .

. . . a membership supported organization of people committed to fostering the growth and development of children from birth through age eight. Membership is open to all who share a desire to serve and act on behalf of the needs and rights of young children.

NAEYC provides . . .

. . . educational services and resources to adults who work with and for children, including

▪ *Young Children, the* Journal for early childhood educators

▪ **Books, posters,** and **brochures** to expand your knowledge and commitment to young children, with topics including infants, curriculum, research, discipline, teacher education, and parent involvement

▪ An **Annual Conference** that brings people from all over the country to share their expertise and advocate on behalf of children and families

▪ **Week of the Young Child** celebrations sponsored by NAEYC Affiliate Groups across the country to call public attention to the needs and rights of children and families

▪ **Insurance plans** for individuals and programs

▪ **Public policy information** for informed advocacy efforts at all levels of government

▪ **For free information about membership, publications, or other NAEYC services** call NAEYC at 800-424-2460 or 202-232-8777 or write to
NAEYC
1834 Connecticut Avenue, N.W.
Washington, DC 20009.

DATE DUE		
NOV 27 1986		
JUL 1 4 1989		
JUL 1 2 1990		